Goju-Ryu Karate-Do

KATA TENSHO

Ancient Form to Modern-Day Application

SHIHAN CHRIS ROWEN

summersdale

KATA TENSHO
Copyright © Chris Rowen, 2005

The right of Chris Rowen to be identified as the author of this work has been asserted in accordance with sections 77 and 78 of the Copyright, Designs and Patents Act 1988.

Condition of Sale
This book is sold subject to the condition that it shall not, by way of trade or otherwise, be lent, re-sold, hired out or otherwise circulated in any form of binding or cover other than that in which it is published and without a similar condition including this condition being imposed on the subsequent publisher.

Summersdale Publishers
46 West Street
Chichester
West Sussex
PO19 1RP

www.summersdale.com

Printed and bound in Great Britain.

ISBN 1 84024 463 1

Please note: The author and the publishers cannot accept any responsibility for any prosecutions or proceedings brought or instituted against any person or body as a result of the use or misuse of the information or any techniques described in this book or any loss, injury or damage caused thereby. Some of the techniques described in this book require high levels of skill and physical fitness. The techniques and methods contained within this book must only be practised by those in good health whilst under qualified supervision.

Goju-Ryu Karate-Do
KATA TENSHO

Ancient Form to Modern-Day Application

ACKNOWLEDGEMENTS

To all sentient beings. To all my teachers past, present and yet to come, my thanks and gratitude. To my peers, my thanks. To my students, thank you for sharing. To Saiko Shihan Yamaguchi Goshi, Toyashima, Togo and Tamaoke Senseis. To Kyoshi Tino Ceberano. To Ide Donno, for my Shinto education. To Akamine Etsuke, Kobudo Teacher of Okinawa who introduced me to that wonderful art of Kobudo. To all at Summersdale Publishing. To John, Tony and Sarah, Steve and all at Shikon. To all Goju practitioners, karateka and martial artists everywhere. To Mertis and Marianne. To Nicky. To Danny Connor. To Mark and all at Richmond. To Sensei Jim McEvoy for assisting in the making of this book. To all the students and teachers of the Bunbukan Institute of Classical Japanese Budo Culture, Iain Abernethy and all the others who have helped and supported throughout the years – you know who you are. To all Members of the Bunbukan Institute of Classical Japanese Budo Culture Mauritian branch, as well as the Welsh, French, German and American branches. To the Nagata family, heartfelt thanks. As always, thanks to Southside Johnny and the Asbury Jukes.

And to you, the reader.

This book is dedicated with great respect to the late Grandmaster Hanshi Yamaguchi Gogen, whose teaching, works and inspiration has certainly influenced my life and, I'm sure, countless others.

CONTENTS

Certificate

No. **1 3 3**   Date **1 SEP. 1984**

This is to certify that

C. J. ROWEN

is a recognized instructor

of Goju-Ryu Karate-Do

Gogen Yamaguchi

Gogen Yamaguchi

President

(hanshi 10th dan)

International Karate-do Goju-kai Association

Taught, graded and awarded teaching certificate in Japan from the legendary tenth dan Gogen Yamaguchi. Direct karate lineage can be traced back to the fifteenth century.

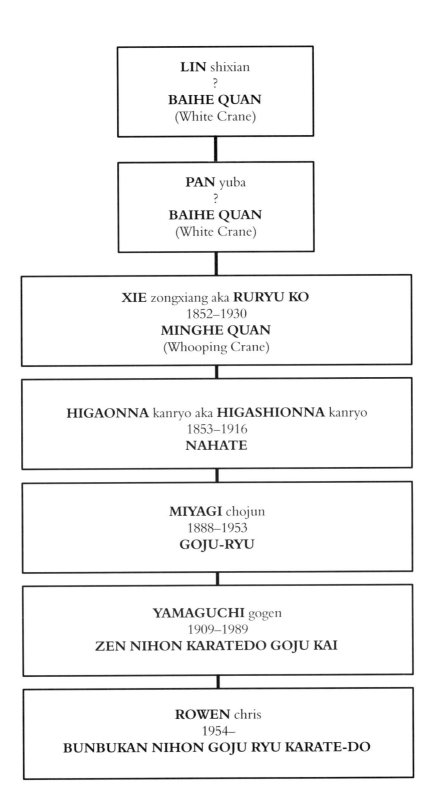

LIN shixian
?
BAIHE QUAN
(White Crane)

PAN yuba
?
BAIHE QUAN
(White Crane)

XIE zongxiang aka **RURYU KO**
1852–1930
MINGHE QUAN
(Whooping Crane)

HIGAONNA kanryo aka **HIGASHIONNA** kanryo
1853–1916
NAHATE

MIYAGI chojun
1888–1953
GOJU-RYU

YAMAGUCHI gogen
1909–1989
ZEN NIHON KARATEDO GOJU KAI

ROWEN chris
1954–
BUNBUKAN NIHON GOJU RYU KARATE-DO

FOREWORD

I am so glad that Chris Rowen has decided to write this book. Along with many other senior karate practitioners, I love Kata Tensho. I was first taught the form by Chris some twenty years ago in his traditional dojo on the top floor of the East West Centre in London. Chris had trained with the late Grandmaster Yamaguchi Gogen in Japan, immersing himself fully in the training, culture and spirit of the Honbu dojo for three years; learning the Japanese language, becoming a Shinto priest, a Shiatsu healer and third dan grade Goju Kai karateka at the same time.

Over those twenty years we have remained firm friends. When I was Chairman of the Governing Body for Karate, Chris was the Secretary and we used his dojo as the office and had many happy hours training there. It was also the location for my first video shoot. Chris visited me many times and when I opened my full-time traditional dojo twelve years ago, Chris consecrated my Shinto shrine and taught me to maintain it properly, visiting it annually for a blessing. He has taught on many of my courses and is a popular instructor.

Chris is a quiet and private man. His spiritual life is integrated into everything he does, so he's not given to promoting himself or demonstrating his amazing martial skill. I have spent years persuading him to pass his knowledge on in a wider sphere for the benefit of the arts. That's why I'm glad to see this book and accompanying DVD, as it lays down the definitive version of the kata for posterity.

Tensho is a beautiful, powerful, adaptable and traditional kata. Since learning it from Chris, I studied the Chinese version, which teaches the 'five animal hands' from Nathan Johnson and have discussed it widely with great martial practitioners such as Steve Arniel, ninth dan exponent of the powerful Kyokushinkai style of karate, and the legendary 'Samurai on the Door' street knockout specialist Dennis Jones – both claim it is a favourite form.

Although I practise the Wado-Ryu style of karate, I incorporated both Sanchin and Kata Tensho into my syllabus after I learned it from Chris – Sanchin to provide the internal system of the martial arts and Tensho to transmit the power and skills learned from Sanchin for a wide variety of uses to include escaping, grappling, striking, locking, blocking and dislocation.

Chris has certainly had an influence on my karate and dojo life. His knowledge of Goju karate – its history, ethos, forms, techniques and their application – is, in my opinion, unsurpassable. This book is a must for any serious martial arts practitioner.

Steve Rowe
Chairman of Shikon Martial Art International, seventh dan

INTRODUCTION

What is 'kata'? In the Japanese language this word means *form*, and in the martial arts specifically this refers to a series of pre-arranged defensive or offensive movements that one can practise by oneself, in which the essence of the art can be realised. In ancient times, dangerous techniques were hidden or incorporated into a kata as a teaching method and as a way of preserving the art.

This book is an introduction to the kata known as Tensho and is for everyone, regardless of style, grade or experience. The chapters are divided in a logical, progressive and modular fashion with instructions on one page and the corresponding pictures opposite in order to demonstrate each movement or technique.

This is the first time ever that a book and DVD has been exclusively produced on the Goju-Ryu kata Tensho. Tensho, which literally means 'turning hands', is one of the two main katas of the Goju-Ryu ('go' means hard, 'ju' means soft, 'ryu' means stream or school) of karate-do. Goju-Ryu itself is one of the four major styles of karate-do (meaning 'way of the empty hand'). In this book, I wish to show the history of this form; from its origins in the fifteenth century, when numerous influences began helping to shape its genesis, to the finished generic form of Tensho.

An ancient martial art known as White Crane, combined with Monk Fist boxing and supported by Nahate, became Goju-Ryu. The same influences affected the development of Kata Tensho from its earlier incarnation as the Chinese form Rokkishu ('six hands'). Legendary practitioners of the art such as Fang Qiniang (daughter of the famous Fang Zhonggong, from the Yongchun countryside in China) are noted for understanding the principles of yielding to and the diversion of power.

I also wish to illustrate the practical concepts of hard (go) and soft (ju) and the interaction of the two. To do so I will need to call on the expertise of karate masters past and present. The Okinawan karate master Kanryo Higaonna (1853–1916) brought elements of the kata from China to Okinawa, where his student, the great master Miyagi Chojun (1888–1953), developed it further, naming it Tensho. This development was then continued by leading experts such as Grandmaster Hanshi Yamaguchi Gogen.

INTRODUCTION

It is the beauty and versatility of this kata that makes it so special. It can be appreciated through the gracefulness of its movement practised slowly and with rhythmic breathing (which has clear health benefits). Its apparently effortless circular movements can redirect and nullify aggressive acts with seemingly minimum effort. In addition, there is the philosophical and humanitarian aspect within the form, and various masters emphasise its importance for moral character and good judgement. Finally, it includes a devastating striking power that, used as a last resort, is unquestionably effective.

By following this book my objective is that you will become proficient in a highly respected martial art, as the chapters lead you step by step in its mastery. As the book's subtitle suggests, the chapters will take you from Kata Tensho's ancient beginnings, starting with the ever-important lesson on 'Etiquette' (historically regarded as the beginning and end of martial arts), through the chapters on 'Standing Basics' and 'Blocks'. Chapter Five is then dedicated to the kata itself in its entirety. Towards the end of the book you will be able to put the new skills into practice and learn how Kata Tensho may be deployed in the modern day.

This is one version of Kata Tensho which includes all the basic components. It is a humble, genuine attempt in a small, imperfect way to share the knowledge of this martial art. I hope you enjoy learning about it as much as I enjoy sharing it.

Shihan C. J. Rowen

KEY POINTS

FIRST PRACTISE SLOWLY AND GET
THE FEEL OF THE TECHNIQUE

BREATHE WITH EACH MOVEMENT

ALWAYS PRACTISE DILIGENTLY

STRENGTH FADES; TECHNIQUE REMAINS

DO NO HARM

WORK WITH PARTNER

Tate Rei
(standing bow)

REI SHIKI
(Etiquette)

In the martial arts the development of the whole person is just as important, if not more so, than the development of one's physical and technical prowess. The practice of etiquette has long been held in high regard. An Okinawan master once wrote that *'karate begins and ends with etiquette'.* In other words, without proper etiquette there is no karate. Etiquette is like karate-do; it is something that is not of any one style, but universal to all styles.

But what *is* karate etiquette?

The dictionary defines etiquette as a *'form of ceremony or decorum; the conventional code of conduct observed between members of the same profession'.* Etiquette is therefore simply a sign of respect; from student to teacher, teacher to student, practitioner to dojo, and dojo to the art itself. This respect should be a permanent trait throughout your karate and in your everyday life.

A karate dojo is one of the few places in the world where people of various backgrounds can come together and try to improve together. For this reason we need etiquette; for both respect and safety. Etiquette is, after all, a built-in safety measure; if we have no respect for others, how can we have respect for ourselves? A lack of respect for your opponent can quite easily result in an accident.

The dojo is the training hall, or more accurately put, the dojo is the place (jo) where one seeks the way (do) to personal achievement through the martial arts.

R1: REI (Standing Bow)
Musubi Dachi – heels together and feet at 45 degrees. Knees bent, back straight and hands at the side of the body. Bow from the waist then return to upright position.

R2: DOWN ONTO LEFT KNEE
Step back with left leg and go down onto the left knee. (Note the foot position: on the ball of the foot.)

R3: DOWN ONTO BOTH KNEES
The right leg follows the same procedure. Feet are placed flat prior to Seiza.

R4: SEIZA (Sit)
Sit in Seiza with the back straight. (Note the position of the feet.) Hands resting on the thighs.

REI SHIKI

R1 Rei

R2 Down onto left knee

R3 Down onto both knees

R4 Seiza

R5: BOW

Place left hand then right hand on the floor and bow. Return to Seiza with the back straight, returning hands onto the thighs – first the right hand and then the left. Repeat the procedure three times.

R6: SEIZA

Return to Seiza. Keep the back straight and the hands resting on the thighs.

R7: PRIOR TO STANDING

Place the right foot forward, keeping on the ball of the foot. Stand up, bringing the right foot back to join the left, and move the heels together in Musabi Dachi (formal stance). Hands are at the side of the body.

R8: BOW AND FORMAL STANCE

Bow from the waist then return to the upright position.

REI SHIKI

R5 Bow

R6 Seiza

R7 Prior to standing

R8 Bow and formal stance

Koken
(wrist block/strike)

KIHON
(Basics)

Kihon is the foundation on which we build our technique. Quite simply if the foundation is weak the technique will not stand. These basic positions should be practised slowly and diligently to begin with.

The hand positions are extremely important. There are two categories of hand position: 'Kaishu', which means *open hand*, of which figure K1 is an example; and 'Heishu', which means *closed hand* or *fist*, of which figure K2 is one example.

Practise first while standing still to familiarise yourself with the position, later progressing to movement.

Note: Koken means to block or strike with the back of a bent wrist in a vertical direction. Seiken means fist.

K1: KAISHU (Open Hand)

Have the hand open. Keep the fingers straight and together.

K2: HEISHU (Closed Hand)

Roll the fingers until the fingertips are pulled tightly into the palm. Place the thumb over the closed fist.

K3: SIDE VIEW

Ensure that there is no bend in the wrist and that the fist is at a 90 degree angle to prevent damage to oneself.

K4: FRONT VIEW

When striking, Kento, or the two largest knuckles, are the actual striking area of the fist.

KIHON

K1 Open hand

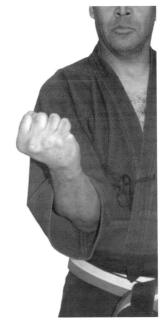

K2 Closed hand

K3 Side view

K4 Front view

K5: KOKEN

The wrist is utilised for blocking or striking in a vertical direction. Fingers point towards the floor using the back of the wrist as the contact area.

K6: SHUTO

Known as the 'knife hand', utilising the edge of the hand to block or strike. Fingers are pulled tightly together and the thumb clenched to the side of the hand.

K7: YOKO KOKEN

Utilised for blocking or striking in a horizontal direction.

K8: UCHI SHOTEI (Inner Palm Heel)

This can be used as a block or a strike. Fingers are pulled back and thumb pulled in tightly. Wrist is bent.

K5 Koken

K6 Shuto

K7 Yoko Koken

K8 Uchi Shotei

K9: HAITO (Ridge Hand)

Fingers are held tightly together. Slightly bent thumb is tucked in to accentuate the muscle at the side of the hand. This is an exceptionally effective striking technique.

K10: BARATE

This back-of-the-fingers strike utilises the back of the hand in a flicking action. Fingers are held tightly together. This is an extremely effective striking method.

(NB: This technique is not as prominent as in former times.)

K11: SANCHIN NO KAMAE (Opening Stance)

Front View

Elbows are a fist distance from the side of the body; the fist is slightly lower than the shoulders. Arms are held slightly to the outside of the body.

K12: SANCHIN NO KAMAE (Opening Stance)

Side View

To commence the movement the right hand passes underneath the left as the arms continue in a circular movement, before pulling and settling with focus into the required position.

K9 Haito

K10 Barate

K11 Sanchin (front view)

K12 Sanchin (side view)

K13: SHOTEI OSHI (Palm Heel)
Jodan (to Upper Level)
This technique can be used to the front. Fingers are pulled back and the thumb is pulled in tightly to accentuate the blocking/striking area of the palm heel.

K14: SHOTEI OSHI (Palm Heel)
Gedan (to Lower Level)
This is exactly the same technique, used in a downward trajectory to the Gedan (lower) area.

K15: NUKITE (Finger Strike)
This is a specialised and very effective striking technique with the back of the hand straight and fingers bent and bunched close together to form a unified striking area. This is then applied with a twisting action. As great care and practice is required to prevent self-injury, this technique is not as well used as in previous times.

K16: NAOTE (Closing Procedure)
At the end of the exercise, the heels are brought together and at the same time the open left hand makes a downward vertical movement as the right hand comes to join it on a horizontal plane. The palm is uppermost and the hands then rotate so that the palms face the body at Gedan level. The hands are then placed at the side of the body and a bow is made.

K13 Shotei Oshi to Jodan

K14 Shotei Oshi to Gedan

K15 Nukite

K16 Naote

Chudan Uke
(closed fist middle block)

UKE
(Blocks)

The practice of Uke reiterates the importance of defensive parameters. If someone is close enough to strike then you have to block or redirect the blow.

Blocks can be performed in one of two ways; either by Heishu (closed hand or fist) or Kaishu (open-handed). The vast majority of blocks in Kata Tensho are performed open-handed.

In the practice of all basic positions and blocks, keep the back straight with the feet a shoulder-width apart and the knees bent. Relax the shoulders and breathe normally. Practise diligently and slowly to begin with. All techniques to be practised on both sides, especially Mawashi Uke.

Master Miyagi Chojun commented on how many Goju-Ryu katas had hand positions similar to Buddhist statues.

Note: In Mawashi Uke the hand which starts out on top remains on top when hands cross and when hands are extended.

CHUDAN UKE
(Closed hand block to middle area)

U1: PREPARATORY
Right hand in Chudan Uke position (middle block). The fist is slightly lower than and to the outside of the shoulder. The elbow is the distance of one fist from the side of the body. The left fist is placed between the body and the elbow with the palm facing downwards.

U2: MID FORM
The left hand moves in a smooth, circular, outward movement. At the midway point the left hand rotates so that the palm is facing upwards.

U3: PULL BACK
As the left fist completes its circular movement with an inwards pulling action, the right fist is pulled back to the side of the body. This movement is carried out smoothly with tension at the end.

U4: SIDE VIEW
Note that the fist is slightly lower than the shoulder and the elbow is a fist-distance from the side of the body.

U1 Preparatory

U2 Mid form

U3 Pull back

U4 Side view

KAISHU CHUDAN HIKI UKE

U5: PREPARATORY KAISHU
(Open hand pulling block to middle area)
The left hand is open in Chudan side position. The right open hand is placed below the left elbow with the palm facing downwards.

U6: MID FORM
The right hand moves in a smooth, circular, outward movement. At the midway point the right hand rotates so that the palm is facing upwards.

U7: PULL BACK
(Accentuated wrist for hook)
As the right hand completes its circular movement, with an inward pulling action the left hand is pulled back to the side of the body. This is done in a smooth movement with tension at the end.

U8: SIDE VIEW
Note the position of the bent hand to help facilitate the pulling/ hooking action.

U5 Preparatory Kaishu

U6 Mid form

U7 Pull back

U8 Side view

KAKE UKE
(Open hand hooking block)

U9: PREPARATORY
The left open hand is in Chudan Uke position. The right open hand is placed under the left elbow with the palm facing upwards.

U10: MID FORM
The right hand moves in a smooth, circular, outward movement. At the midway point the right wrist rotates so that the palm is facing downwards.

U11: PULLING AND BLOCKING
At the same time as the right open hand completes its circular movement with an inward pulling action, the left open hand covers the solar plexus with a downward action. This is a smooth movement with tension at the end.

U12: SIDE VIEW
Note that the hand covers the solar plexus as a protective measure.

U9 Preparatory

U10 Mid form

U11 Pulling and blocking

U12 Side view

USHIRO KAKE UKE
(Inner hooking block)

U13: PREPARATORY

The right hand is in Kake Uke position with the palm facing downwards. The left hand is open and covering the solar plexus.

U14: MID FORM

The right wrist rotates with a small circular movement of the elbow so that the palm is now uppermost. A smooth hooking action is achieved by allowing the fingers to fold inwards. These movements should be performed with a fluid action and require practice!

U15: PULL/REDIRECT

The right hand continues its circular hooking movement. This movement is designed to redirect and unbalance an opponent. The left hand protects the solar plexus.

U16: SIDE VIEW

Note the inward positioning of the hand for hooking and redirecting.

U13 Preparatory

U14 Mid form

U15 Pull/redirect

U16 Side view

MAWASHI UKE
(Circular block)

U17: PREPARATORY
Have the hand open in Chudan Uke position with the palm facing you. The left open hand is placed underneath the right elbow with the palm facing down.

U18: MID FORM
The right hand moves downwards in a circular motion, passing close to the body to perform a right open hand lower block. Meanwhile the left hand passes in a circular motion and an upward direction to perform a left open hand middle block.

U19: CROSS HANDS
The hands continue in a circular movement until the hands align at chest height, with the right hand uppermost. Cross hands and a double inner hooking block is commenced.

U20: PULL BACK
Pull back the hands to the side of the body. Palms are facing upwards.

U17 Preparatory

U18 Mid form

U19 Cross hands

U20 Pull back

U21: ROTATION

Turn the palms so the right hand is pointing upwards whilst the left hand points downwards.

U22: EXTENDED

Extend the palms forward, ensuring the distance between the side of the body and the elbow is one fist in width.

U23: END POSITION

Front view
Note the distance of the elbows from the body.

U24: END POSITION

Side view
Note how the heels of the palms are an equal distance from the body.

NB: PRACTISE MAWASHI UKE REGULARLY ON BOTH SIDES FOR SMOOTH EXECUTION.

U21 Rotation

U22 Extended

U23 End position (front view)

U24 End position (side view)

Sanchin Dachi
(hour glass stance)

DACHI
(Stances)

Stances are very important. They give us stability as well as a strong starting point for movement. Kata Tensho consists of very few stances, Sanchin Dachi (the hour glass stance) being the most prominent. This gives a very strong, stable base. For all stances, keep the knees bent and the back straight. Practise your movements forwards and backwards regularly so that you can move freely in a balanced way and are able to marry technique with movement. But remember to start slowly – there are aspects of twisting and gripping to master.

D1: MUSUBI DACHI (Formal Stance)

Heels together, knees normal, feet pointing at 45 degrees. This is the formal respectful stance at the beginning and end of kata. Also used prior to bowing.

D2: HEIKO DACHI / YOI DACHI (Ready Stance)

Feet are a shoulder width apart. Knees are slightly bent. This the ready position of awareness. Moving into the stance, the fists press down, the pelvis tilts upwards and the toes grip. This movement combined with breathing is sometimes referred to as 'heaven and earth meeting'.

D3: PREPARATION FOR SANCHIN DACHI (Hour Glass Stance)

Place the right foot in front of the left foot with the left foot in line with the left shoulder, facing straight ahead. Then move the right foot across to be in alignment with the right shoulder so feet are now a shoulder-width apart.

D4: SANCHIN DACHI (Hour Glass Stance)

With the right foot now one foot's length in front of the left, twist the heels of the feet slightly outwards, which will turn the toes inwards. Grip the floor with the toes and bend the knees so that the weight is evenly distributed.

DACHI

D1 Musubi Dachi

D2 Heiko Dachi / Yoi Dachi

D3 Preparation for Sanchin Dachi

D4 Sanchin Dachi

RIGHT SANCHIN DACHI

D5: PREPARATION FOR STANCE CHANGE
To move forward in left Sanchin Dachi, straighten the front foot so that the toes are pointing to the front. Keep the knees bent.

D6: MID FORM
Move the left foot forward in a smooth semi-circular action, making sure not to cross over the midline. Keep the soles of the feet firmly on the floor.

D7: COMPLETION OF FORWARD MOVEMENT
The left foot has now completed the semi-circular movement into left Sanchin Dachi.

D8: GRIPPING THE FLOOR
At completion, adjust the feet so that the toes point slightly inwards. Grip the floor with the toes. To move into right Sanchin Dachi, repeat the process on the opposite side.

NB: MOVEMENT SHOULD BE PERFORMED SMOOTHLY FROM ONE STANCE TO ANOTHER WITH NO PERCEPTION OF DIFFERENCE IN HEIGHT, WHICH WOULD INDICATE BEING OFF BALANCE IN SOME WAY.

D5 Preparation for stance change

D6 Mid form

*D7 Completion of
forward movement*

D8 Gripping the floor

BACKWARD MOVEMENT

D9: PREPARATION FOR STANCE CHANGE

To move backward from right Sanchin Dachi, slightly straighten the right foot and keep knees bent.

D10: MID FORM

Move the right foot back in a smooth semi-circular action, making sure not to cross over the midline. Keep the soles of the foot firmly on the floor.

D11: COMPLETION OF BACKWARD MOVEMENT

The right foot has now completed the semi-circular movement into left Sanchin.

D12: GRIPPING THE FLOOR

Adjust the feet so that the toes point slightly inwards. At completion, grip the floor with the toes. Repeat the process on the opposite side.

Practise forward and backward movement regularly, keeping the knees bent. Soles of the feet must be kept firmly on the floor and gripping with the toes.

DACHI

D9 Preparation for stance change

D10 Mid form

*D11 Completion of
backward movement*

D12 Gripping the floor

KATA TENSHO:
A PICTORIAL HISTORY

All photographs from author's private collection

不動妙

FUDO MYOO
Guardian Deity of Japanese Martial Artists

MIYAGI CHOJUN (1888–1953)
The great karate master of Okinawa and founder of Goju-Ryu karate-do

HANSHI YAMAGUCHI GOGEN (1909–1989)
The great karate master of Japan

AKAMINE ETSUKE (1925–1999)
The great Kobudo master of Okinawa

OMIYA HACHIMAN SHRINE, JAPAN
Author kata training

AUTHOR'S LONDON DOJO
Rooftop training with students: Kaishu techniques

AUTHOR'S LONDON DOJO
Maki Wara training

AUTHOR'S LONDON DOJO
Application with student

OMIYA HACHIMAN SHRINE, JAPAN
Author kata training

BUNBUKAN MAURITIAN BRANCH
Junior members' summer Gassuku (training camp)

BUNBUKAN MAURITIAN BRANCH
Members' summer Gassuku

BEACH TRAINING IN MAURITIUS
Bunbukan senior members' Gassuku: Heishu kata

BEACH TRAINING IN MAURITIUS
Bunbukan senior members' Gassuku: Kaishu kata

**BUNBUKAN MAURITIAN
BRANCH SENIOR INSTRUCTORS**
Sensei Danny and Sensei Rauf

OKINAWA BEACH SCENE WITH SAI

OMIYA HACHIMAN SHRINE, JAPAN
Author kata training

ENSO
Enso means circle. This is representative of
the cyclic nature of life and training.

Nihon Uke
(double hooking block)

KATA TENSHO
(Turning Hands Form)

The Embusen or basic direction of Kata Tensho is simple: moving forwards and backwards in a straight line. Aim for a smooth progression, combining movement and technique. Practise repeatedly, breathing in a controlled manner with each movement.

When breathing through the nose make short, progressive inhalations. When alternating between inhalation and exhalation do so using a balanced and smooth style.

When performing Mawashi Uke in the kata from the preparatory position, the hand on top corresponds with the rear leg. This hand starts, crosses and ends in the top position.

KT1: REI (Standing Bow)

KT2: YOI (Ready Position)
Breathe in through the nose and out through the mouth.

KT3: RIGHT SANCHIN
Step forward into a right Sanchin Dachi. The right arm passes under the left as you move forward into right (Migi) Sanchin, Chudan No Kamae. *Breathing in through the nose.*

KT4: WITHDRAW LEFT FIST
Withdraw the left (Hidari) fist to the side of the body. *Breathing in through the nose.*

KATA TENSHO

KT1 Rei

KT2 Yoi

KT3 Right (Migi) Sanchin No Kamae

KT4 Withdraw left (Hidari) fist

KT5: RIGHT KAISHU HIKI UKE

Open hand (palm is uppermost). Bend the wrist to perform a right Kaisho Chudan Hiki Uke (open hand pulling block). *Breathing in through the nose.*

KT6: RIGHT KAKE UKE

Rotate the wrist to perform a right Chudan Kake Uke (hooking block). *Breathing in through the nose.*

KT7: RIGHT USHIRO KAKE UKE

Rotate the wrist to perform a right Chudan Ushiro Kake Uke with a circular action (inner hooking block). *Breathing in through the nose.*

KT8: WITHDRAW

Pull the right hand back to the side of the body with the palm uppermost.

MOVEMENTS KT5–KT8 ARE PERFORMED IN A SMOOTH, CONTINUOUS, CIRCULAR ACTION, BREATHING IN THROUGH THE NOSE.

KT5 Right Kaishu Hiki Uke

KT6 Right Kake Uke

KT7 Right Ushiro Kake Uke

KT8 Withdraw

KT9: ROTATE RIGHT PALM

Rotate the right hand with the palm facing outwards and fingers uppermost. *Breathing in through the nose.*

KT10: SHOTEI OSHI TO JODAN

With the right hand perform a Jodan Shotei Oshi (palm heel push) to the front upper area with the arm extended but a slight bend in the elbow. *Breathing out through the mouth.*

KT11: WITHDRAW

Make a large circular motion. Withdraw the right hand back to the side of the body prior to Shotei Oshi to Gedan. *Breathing in through the nose.*

KT12: SHOTEI OSHI TO GEDAN

Perform Shotei Oshi to Gedan (palm heel push) to the lower area. *Breathing out through the mouth.*

MOVEMENTS KT9–KT12 ARE PERFORMED IN A SMOOTH, FLOWING, CONTINUOUS ACTION.

KT9 Rotate right palm

KT10 Shotei Oshi to Jodan

KT11 Withdraw

KT12 Shotei Oshi to Gedan

KT13: POSITION PRIOR TO KOKEN

Rotate the wrist so that the fingers are pointing downwards with the back of the wrist facing the front. Place the thumb in the middle of the fingers and bunch the fingers tightly together. *Breathing in through the nose.*

KT14: KOKEN UKE

In a smooth movement with tension, bring the hand upwards, folding the fingers to perform Chudan Koken Uke (wrist block). *Breathing in through the nose.*

KT15: SHUTO OTOSHI UKE

In a smooth motion, perform Chudan Shuto Otoshi Uke (knife hand downward block). *Breathing out through the mouth.*

KT16: YOKO KOKEN UKE

In a flowing action, perform Chudan Yoko Koken Uke (outer wrist block). *Breathing in through the nose.*

MOVEMENTS KT13–KT16 ARE PERFORMED IN A SMOOTH, FLOWING, CONTINUOUS ACTION.

KT13 Postion prior to Koken

KT14 Koken Uke

KT15 Shuto Otoshi Uke

KT16 Yoko Koken Uke

KT17: UCHI SHOTEI UKE

In a flowing action, perform a Chudan Uchi Shotei Uke (inner palm heel block). *Breathing out through the mouth.*

KT18: LEFT SANCHIN DACHI CHUDAN UKE

Step forward into a left Sanchin Dachi and perform a left Chudan Uke. *Breathing in through the nose.*

KT19: KAISHU HIKI UKE

Open hand. Bend the wrist to perform a left Kaishu Chudan Hiki Uke in a circular movement. *Breathing in through the nose.*

KT20: KAKE UKE

Rotate the wrist to perform a left Chudan Kake Uke. *Breathing in through the nose.*

MOVEMENTS KT17–KT20 ARE PERFORMED IN A SMOOTH, CONTINUOUS, CIRCULAR ACTION.

KT17 Uchi Shotei Uke

KT18 Left Sanchin Dachi Chudan Uke

KT19 Kaishu Hiki Uke

KT20 Kake Uke

KT21: USHIRO KAKE UKE

Rotate the wrist to perform a left Chudan Ushiro Kake Uke with a circular motion. *Breathing in through the nose.*

KT22: WITHDRAW

Pull the left hand back to the side of the body with the palm uppermost. *Breathing in through the nose.*

KT23: ROTATE LEFT PALM

Rotate the left hand with the palm facing outwards and fingers uppermost. Breathing in through the nose.

KT24: SHOTEI OSHI TO JODAN

With the left hand perform a Jodan Shotei Oshi to the front with the arm extended but a slight bend in the elbow. Breathing out through the mouth.

MOVEMENTS KT21–KT24 ARE PERFORMED IN A SMOOTH, CONTINUOUS, CIRCULAR ACTION.

KT21 Ushiro Kake Uke

KT22 Withdraw

KT23 Rotate left palm

KT24 Shotei Oshi to Jodan

KT25: WITHDRAW

Make a circular motion and withdraw the left hand back to the side of the body (prior to Shotei Oshi to Gedan). *Breathing in through the nose.*

KT26: SHOTEI OSHI TO GEDAN

Perform Shotei Oshi to Gedan. *Breathing out through the mouth.*

KT27: POSITION PRIOR TO KOKEN UKE

Rotate the wrist so that the fingers are pointing downwards and the back of the wrist is facing the front. Place thumb in the middle of the fingers and bunch the fingers tightly together. *Breathing in through the nose.*

KT28: KOKEN UKE

In a smooth movement with tension, bring the hand upwards folding the fingers to perform Chudan Koken Uke. *Breathing in through the nose.*

MOVEMENTS KT25–KT28 ARE PERFORMED IN A SMOOTH, CONTINUOUS, CIRCULAR ACTION.

KATA TENSHO

KT29 Shuto Otoshi Uke

KT30 Yoko Koken Uke

KT31 Uchi Shotei Uke

KT32 Sanchin No Kamae

KT33: DOUBLE KAISHU HIKI UKE

Perform a double Kaishu Chudan Hiki Uke in a circular movement. *Breathing in through the nose.*

KT34: DOUBLE KAKE UKE

Rotate the wrist to perform a double Chudan Kake Uke. *Breathing in through the nose.*

KT35: DOUBLE USHIRO KAKE UKE

Rotate the wrists to perform a double Chudan Ushiro Kake Uke with a circular action. *Breathing in through the nose.*

KT36: WITHDRAW

Pull the hands back to the side of the body with the palms uppermost. *Breathing in through the nose.*

MOVEMENTS KT33–KT36 ARE PERFORMED IN A SMOOTH, CONTINUOUS, CIRCULAR ACTION.

KATA TENSHO

KT33 Double Kaishu Hiki Uke

KT34 Double Kake Uke

KT35 Double Ushiro Kake Uke

KT36 Withdraw

KT37: ROTATE BOTH PALMS

Rotate the hands with the palms facing outwards and fingers uppermost. *Breathing in through the nose.*

KT38: DOUBLE SHOTEI OSHI TO JODAN

With both hands perform Jodan Shotei Oshi to the front. The arms should be extended with a slight bend in the elbows. *Breathing out through the mouth.*

KT39: WITHDRAW

Make circular motions and withdraw both hands back to the side of the body prior to performing Shotei Oshi to Gedan. *Breathing in through the nose.*

KT40: DOUBLE SHOTEI OSHI TO GEDAN

Perform a double Shotei Oshi to Gedan. *Breathing out through the mouth.*

MOVEMENTS KT37–KT40 ARE PERFORMED IN A SMOOTH, CONTINUOUS, CIRCULAR ACTION.

KATA TENSHO

KT37 Rotate both palms

KT38 Double Shotei Oshi to Jodan

KT39 Withdraw

KT40 Double Shotei Oshi to Gedan

KT41: POSITION PRIOR TO DOUBLE KOKEN UKE
Rotate the wrists so that the fingers are facing downwards with the backs of the wrists facing the front. Place thumbs in the middle of the fingers and bunch fingers tightly together. *Breathing in through the nose.*

KT42: DOUBLE KOKEN UKE
In a smooth movement with tension, bring the hands upwards folding the fingers to perform double Koken Uke. *Breathing in through the nose.*

KT43: DOUBLE SHUTO OTOSHI UKE
In a smooth motion, perform a double Chudan Shuto Otoshi Uke. *Breathing out through the mouth.*

KT44: DOUBLE YOKO KOKEN UKE
In a flowing action, perform a double Chudan Yoko Koken Uke. *Breathing in through the nose.*

MOVEMENTS KT41–KT44 ARE PERFORMED IN A SMOOTH, CONTINUOUS, CIRCULAR ACTION.

KT41 Position prior to Double Koken Uke

KT42 Double Koken Uke

KT43 Double Shuto Otoshi Uke

KT44 Double Yoko Koken Uke

KT45: DOUBLE UCHI SHOTEI UKE

In a flowing action, perform double Chudan Uchi Shotei Uke. *Breathing out through the mouth.*

KT46: BACKS OF HANDS TOGETHER

Extend the arms and place the backs of the hands together. *Breathing in through the nose.*

KT47: WITHDRAW

Withdraw hands to the side of the body with the palms uppermost. *Breathing in through the nose.*

KT48: DOUBLE NUKITE

Lower the hands to waist level. Push the arms forward until the elbows are at the front of the body. Rotate arms to perform a double Chudan Nukite (finger strike) with tension. *Breathing out through the mouth.*

MOVEMENTS KT45–KT48 ARE PERFORMED IN A SMOOTH, CONTINUOUS, CIRCULAR ACTION.

KATA TENSHO

KT45 Double Uchi Shotei Uke

KT46 Backs of hands together

KT47 Withdraw

KT48 Double Nukite

KT49: BACKS OF HANDS TOGETHER

Step back into left Sanchin Dachi. Place the backs of the hands together. *Breathing in through the nose.*

KT50: WITHDRAW

Withdraw hands to the side of body with palms uppermost. *Breathing in through the nose.*

KT51: DOUBLE NUKITE

Lower hands to waist level and push arms forwards until elbows are at the front of the body. Rotate arms to perform a double Chudan Nukite with tension. *Breathing out through the mouth.*

KT52: BACKS OF HANDS TOGETHER

Step back into right Sanchin Dachi and place the backs of the hands together. *Breathing in through the nose.*

MOVEMENTS KT49–KT52 ARE PERFORMED IN A SMOOTH, CONTINUOUS, CIRCULAR ACTION.

KT49 Backs of hands together

KT50 Withdraw

KT51 Double Nukite

KT52 Backs of hands together

KT53: WITHDRAW

Withdraw hands to side of the body with palms uppermost. *Breathing in through the nose.*

KT54: DOUBLE NUKITE

Lower hands to waist level and push arms forwards until the elbows are at the front of the body. Rotate the arms to perform a double Nukite with tension. *Breathing out through the mouth.*

KT55: PREPARATORY POSITION FOR MAWASHI UKE

Step back into left Sanchin Dachi with right hand uppermost in a preparatory position for Mawashi Uke (circular block). *Breathing in through the nose.*

KT56: MAWASHI UKE IN PROGRESS

Part way through Mawashi Uke in a circular motion, the left hand is moving upwards to block the middle area, whilst the right hand is moving downwards to block the lower area. *Breathing in through the nose.*

MOVEMENTS KT53–KT56 ARE PERFORMED IN A SMOOTH, CONTINUOUS, CIRCULAR ACTION.

KATA TENSHO

KT53 Withdraw

KT54 Double Nukite

*KT55 Preparatory position
for Mawashi Uke*

KT56 Mawashi Uke in progress

KT57: DOUBLE USHIRO KAKE UKE
Continue circular action double Ushiro Chudan Kake Uke. *Breathing in through the nose.*

KT58: WITHDRAW
Withdraw hands to side of the body with palms uppermost. *Breathing in through the nose.*

KT59: PALMS TURNING OUTWARDS
Twist palms so that they are facing outwards. The right fingers of the right palm should be pointing upwards and the fingers of the left palm should be pointing downwards. *Breathing in through the nose.*

KT60: SHOTEI OSHI TO JODAN AND GEDAN
Double Shotei Oshi to Jodan and Gedan with tension. Elbows are a fist distance from the side of the body. *Breathing out through the mouth.*

MOVEMENTS KT57–KT60 ARE PERFORMED IN A SMOOTH, CONTINUOUS, CIRCULAR ACTION.

KT57 Double Ushiro Kake Uke

KT58 Withdraw

KT59 Palms turning outwards

KT60 Shotei Oshi
to Jodan and Gedan

KT61: PREPARATORY POSITION FOR MAWASHI UKE
Step back into right Sanchin Dachi with the left hand uppermost ready and prepared for Mawashi Uke. *Breathing in through the nose.*

KT62: CIRCULAR ACTION IN PROGRESS
Part way through Mawashi Uke, in a circular action move the right hand upwards to block middle area, whilst left hand should be moving downwards to block lower area. *Breathing in through the nose.*

KT63: DOUBLE USHIRO KAKE UKE
Continue circular action to perform a double Ushiro Chudan Kake Uke. *Breathing in through the nose.*

KT64: WITHDRAW
Withdraw hands to the side of the body with palms uppermost. *Breathing in through the nose.*

MOVEMENTS KT61–KT64 ARE PERFORMED IN A SMOOTH, CONTINUOUS, CIRCULAR ACTION.

*KT61 Preparatory position
for Mawashi Uke*

KT62 Circular action in progress

KT63 Double Ushiro Kake Uke

KT64 Withdraw

KT65: PALMS FACING OUTWARDS
Twist the palms so that they are facing outwards with the left-hand fingers pointing upwards and the right-hand fingers pointing downwards. *Breathing in through the nose.*

KT66: DOUBLE SHOTEI OSHI TO JODAN AND GEDAN
Double Shotei Oshi to Jodan and Gedan with tension. The elbows are a fist distance from the side of the body. *Breathing out through the mouth.*

KT67: NAOTE
The left open hand drops vertically as the right open hand moves horizontally to meet it. At the same time bring the right heel to meet the left heel. Palms are rotated to face the body. *Breathe in through the nose when hands and heels meet and again when palms are rotated.*

KT68: REI
Palms to the side of the body. Maintain Zanshin (awareness). Rei (bow) and breathe out. Return to formal position.

MOVEMENTS KT65–KT68 ARE PERFORMED IN A SMOOTH, CONTINUOUS, CIRCULAR ACTION.

KT65 Palms facing outwards

*KT66 Double Shotei Oshi
to Jodan and Gedan*

KT67 Naote

KT68 Rei

Kaishu Chudan Hiki Uke
(open hand pulling block to middle area)

TRAINING WITH PARTNER: FLOW DRILLS

Training with a partner and the use of flow drills are essential for understanding Kata Tensho. It is important to emphasise the fact that you work *with* your partner rather than *against* him or her. Training is not a competition using strength against strength – remember, *strength fades, technique remains.* As you train, try to be aware of and feel the intricacies of pulling, hooking, redirecting and unbalancing.

With practice and through the application of these exercises, your understanding and performance of Kata Tensho should improve greatly.

CHUDAN UKE

TP1: PREPARATORY

Face partner in Heiko Dachi (parallel stance). *A* places right fist with the palm down under the left elbow. *B* places left fist under his/her right elbow.

TP2: CHUDAN UKE – MIDWAY

Partners simultaneously make a smooth, circular, outward movement. At the midway point, fists rotate so that the palms are facing upwards.

TP3: PULLING

When fists complete their circular movement and contact is made, they are moved outwards to lock onto each other prior to inward pulling action.

TP4: CLOSE UP

Once contact is made, a slight pulling action is performed to check the balance of each partner. The process is smooth and continuous, with tension at the end of the technique. Repeat on the other side.

B   A

TP1 Preparatory

TP2 Chudan Uke – midway

TP3 Pulling

TP4 Close up

KAISHU CHUDAN HIKI UKE

TP5: PREPARATORY
Face partner in Heiko Dachi (parallel stance). *A* places right open hand palm down under left elbow. *B* places left open hand down under his/her right elbow.

TP6: MIDWAY
Partners simultaneously move hands in a smooth circular outward movement. At the midway point, the hands rotate so palms are facing upwards.

TP7: PULLING
When open hands complete their circular movement and contact is made, palms are moved outwards to lock onto each other prior to an inward pulling action.

TP8: CLOSE UP
Once contact is made, a slight pulling action is performed to check the balance of each partner. The process is smooth and continuous with tension at the end of the technique. Repeat on the other side.

TRAINING WITH PARTNER

B   A

TP5 Preparatory

TP6 Midway

TP7 Pulling

TP8 Close up

CHUDAN KAKE UKE

TP9: PREPARATORY

Face partner in Heiko Dachi (parallel stance). *A* places right open hand under left elbow. *B* places left open hand down under his/her right elbow.

TP10: MIDWAY

Partners simultaneously move hands in a smooth, circular, outward movement. At midway point the hands rotate so palms are facing downwards.

TP11: PULLING

The open hands complete their circular movement and contact is made. Keep close contact and lock on to each other prior to a downward oblique pulling action.

TP12: CLOSE UP

Once contact is established, a slight pulling action is performed to check the balance of each partner. The process is again smooth and continuous with tension at the end.

B   A

TP9 Preparatory

TP10 Midway

TP11 Pulling

TP12 Close up

USHIRO CHUDAN KAKE UKE

TP13: PREPARATORY

Face partner in Heiko Dachi (parallel stance). Both partners have made right Kake Uke with their palms facing down and both have their left hands covering their solar plexus.

TP14: MIDWAY

Partners simultaneously make a smooth, circular, inward movement. At the midway point, the wrists rotate in a small circular motion with the elbow, so that the palms are now uppermost.

TP15: PULLING

When the open hands complete the circular movement and make contact with each other, keep the contact close and lock together prior to carrying out an inward and oblique pulling action.

TP16: CLOSE UP

Once contact is established, a slight pulling action is performed to check the balance of each partner. The process is smooth and continuous with tension at the end.

TRAINING WITH PARTNER

B   A

TP13 Preparatory

TP14 Midway

TP15 Pulling

TP16 Close up

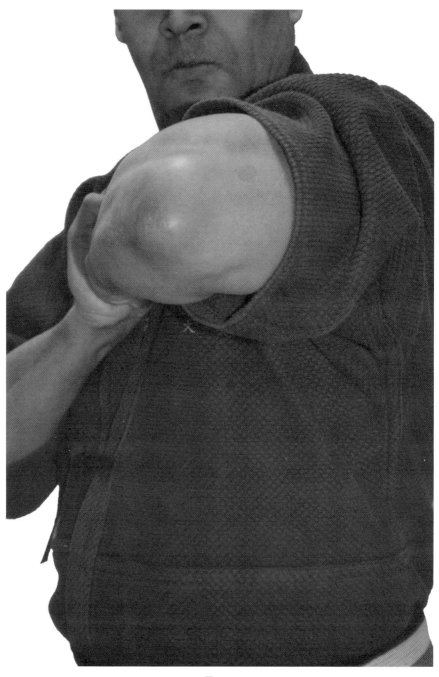

Empi
(elbow)

RENROKU-WAZA
(Combination Technical Drill)

Renroku-Waza is a useful exercise whilst working with a partner that utilises defensive, offensive and escape techniques, combined with elements of pulling, pushing, twisting, locking and redirection.

Begin slowly and work closely with your partner in order to get the feel of the movements involved, using a flowing style.

Do no harm. Be aware of your strength.

KATA TENSHO

RW1: KAISHU UKE

A faces partner in Heiko Dachi (parallel stance). Partners pull with right Kaishu Chudan Hiki Uke. Left hands are covering the solar plexus.

RW2: KAKE UKE

Maintaining close contact, wrists simultaneously rotate into right Kake Uke with a downward pulling action.

RW3: ELBOW STRIKE AND BLOCK

A quickly folds elbow into right Yoko Empi (side elbow strike). *B* simultaneously blocks with a left Kaishu Uke (open hand block). Right hands are still in contact with each other.

RW4: LIFTING THE ELBOW

B pushes *A*'s elbow upwards prior to pivoting to his right and administering a wrist lock.

RENROKU-WAZA

A   B
RW1 Kaishu Uke

RW2 Kake Uke

RW3 Elbow strike and block

RW4 Lifting the elbow

RW5: PUSHING DOWNWARDS

B completes pivoting to the right and pushes *A*'s elbow downwards.

RW6: PULLING OFF BALANCE

A quickly brings his right hand in towards his body whilst simultaneously grabbing *B*'s right elbow (with his left hand), and bringing it forcefully downwards to bring him off balance.

RW7: PUSH UP AND WRIST LOCK

A's left hand now pushes *B*'s elbow upwards whilst simultaneously applying a wrist lock prior to pivoting to his right.

RW8: PIVOT AND PUSH DOWN

A pivots quickly to his right and pushes *B*'s elbow downwards whilst the wrist lock is maintained. The process is then repeated on opposite sides in a flowing manner.

A   B
RW5 Pushing downwards   *RW6 Pulling off balance*

RW7 Push up and wrist lock   *RW8 Pivot and push down*

Ashi Barai
(foot sweep)

TENSHO APPLICATIONS

'Those who learn the great art of karate should help others, never seek trouble and refrain from fighting'

Master Kanryo Higashionna (1853–1916)

It is the apparently simple and innocuous aspect of Kata Tensho that makes it so effective. Here are just some of the many and varied applications from this martial art.

Remember, *do no harm*. Work with your partner and consider the principle of 'combined responsibility'.

TA1: KAISHU UKE
Face partner in Heiko Dachi (parallel stance). Partner *A* blocks *B*'s punch with a left Kaishu Uke (open hand block).

TA2: KAKE UKE
A steps forward, controlling *B*'s arm with his left arm whilst simultaneously carrying out a right hand Kake Uke to *B*'s neck.

TA3: PULL DOWNWARD
A sinks his weight and quickly pulls his hands in a downward and oblique direction, pulling *B* off balance.

TA4: EXECUTE
A quickly raises his body, simultaneously snapping his forearm under his opponent's chin.

TENSHO APPLICATIONS

A   B

TA1 Kaishu Uke   TA2 Kake Uke

TA3 Pull downward   TA4 Execute

TA5: KAISHU UKE BLOCK

A utilises Kaishu Uke (right open hand block) against *B*'s Haito (ridge hand strike). The Kaishu Uke is performed quickly in a circular manner with the body twisting.

TA6: REDIRECT

A continues the circular sweeping action to redirect *B*'s strike.

TA7: HAITO

A swiftly twists body in opposite direction whilst simultaneously striking a left Haito (to the neck) and further redirecting *B*'s strike.

TA8: KOKEN

A's right hand continues to sweep *B*'s hand away, creating space for a left hand circular action to commence Koken strike. This is performed in a fast, circular, sweeping action.

TENSHO APPLICATIONS

TA5 Kaishu Uke Block   *TA6 Redirect*

TA7 Haito   *TA8 Koken*

TA9: KOKEN
A's left Koken (wrist strike) makes a circular whipping action and establishes contact with opponent's midsection, causing opponent to double up.

TA10: KOKEN EXTENDED
A pulls left wrist away swiftly prior to Ashi Barai (foot sweep).

TA11: MID ASHI BARAI
A twists his body at the same time, having brought his right hand round in a circular action to rest on his opponent's back, simultaneously applying Ashi Barai (foot sweep).

TA12: TAKE-DOWN
Whilst the opponent's leg is swept in one direction, the hand pushes the body in another. *A* turns to maintain Zanshin (awareness).

ALL MOVEMENTS ARE PERFORMED IN A FAST, SWEEPING ACTION.

A   B

TA9 Koken   *TA10 Koken extended*

TA11 Mid Ashi Barai   *TA12 Take-down*

SHOTEI

TA13: PREPARATORY
A faces partner in Heiko Dachi (parallel stance). From a pulling action, B prepares to strike.

TA14: BLOCK
B punches and A begins to block with his left inner forearm in an inward circular action whilst twisting body to the side.

TA15: CONTINUATION
A continues the inward forearm block and redirects B's strike.

TA16: SHOTEI STRIKE
A's left arm continues in a circular action, simultaneously twisting to the front and striking with Shotei.

ALL MOVEMENTS ARE PERFORMED SWIFTLY.

TENSHO APPLICATIONS

B A

TA13 Preparatory   *TA14 Block*

TA15 Continuation   *TA16 Shotei Strike*

TA17: PREPARATORY
A faces partner *B* in Heiko Dachi (parallel stance). *A* blocks *B*'s strike with a right downward elbow block whilst twisting the body.

TA18: MIDWAY
A slides the right elbow downwards prior to wrist control.

TA19: BLOCK AND STRIKE
Whilst simultaneously controlling *B*'s right hand, *A* strikes quickly with the left knife hand strike to *B*'s upper arm.

TA20: CONTROL AND STRIKE
A maintains control of *B*'s wrist and simultaneously strikes directly and forcefully with the left thumb.

ALL MOVEMENTS ARE FAST AND FLOWING.

B   A

TA17 Preparatory   *TA18 Midway*

TA19 Block and strike   *TA20 Control and strike*

TA21: WRIST GRAB
A's wrist is grabbed by *B*.

TA22: CIRCLE
A swiftly and forcefully makes an inner circular motion and applies a wrist lock.

TA23: PRESSURE
A applies more rotation to *B*'s wrist and more power is applied.

TA24: FORCE DOWN
A drives his opponent forcefully to the floor in an oblique downward direction.

TENSHO APPLICATIONS

A   B

TA21 Wrist grab   TA22 Circle

TA23 Pressure   TA24 Force down

AFTERWORD

Bunbukan Philosophy

After the passing of Hanshi Yamaguchi Gogen and after many years' training, the Bunbukan Institute of Classical Japanese Budo Culture was formed in the early 1990s to preserve and pass on certain elements of the wonderful art of karate-do and related subjects. All knowledge should be shared; yet, as I always say to my students, *with knowledge comes responsibility*.

When a person first starts to study with the Bunbukan, communication and explanation are of great importance. Courtesy and etiquette are the first subjects that are tackled. It is important that courtesy and etiquette are implemented not only as a basis for good relationships but also as a conduit for two-way communication. It is often said that people hear but do not truly understand. This is sometimes due to their bringing pre-conceived ideas (i.e. karate is a violent, bullying, wild, fighting art) into the learning process where sometimes those ideas cloud one's judgement and lead to misconception. Because of the nature of the martial art, this could lead to harm to others as well as to oneself. To guard against this, etiquette is, in effect, a built-in safety measure. Showing respect to others is also a form of respect for ourselves as well as for the art we practise.

One of the major lessons in Bunbukan teaching is not to do harm to others or oneself. It is not a violent or destructive art; in fact, quite the opposite. The 'bu' ideogram in Bun*bu*kan means literally to 'stop fighting'. It is important to have a structure in place to explain these concepts clearly. One aspect of this of which I wish to write briefly is that of *sit, stand, walk*. By teaching in this way, people learn a logical, progressive syllabus.

To *sit* is the first step. In Japanese culture, sitting is not sitting as we know it, i.e. on a chair. It is a kneeling position, which is adopted for formal interaction and meditation practice. At first it can be quite uncomfortable; people begin to fidget and the mind starts to wander. After practice it becomes less uncomfortable and the mind becomes more stable.

AFTERWORD

There is an old saying in the martial arts: *'If you can't sit, how can you stand? If you can't stand how can you move? And if you can't move how can you even think of conflict or how can you avoid it?'*

After sitting, people learn to *stand* (in other words, learn stances) and then go on to learn the basics of the form. These commence with blocking or a non-aggressive means of protecting oneself against external aggression. As the karate master Miyagi Chojun stated, the goal is *'not to hit, not to be hit'* – emphasising the moral precepts and responsibility instilled within the art.

After this, we look at movement; the concept of distance and non-confrontational awareness. This is just a starting point on the learning journey. It was once said that it takes a thousand days to forge the spirit and ten thousand days to polish it. It is an ongoing process, and one that is important to pass on to others in the correct manner.

A student once asked a Zen priest the secret of life. The priest answered, *'When sitting, just sit. When walking, just walk. But most of all… don't wobble.'*

Shihan C. J. Rowen

The Bunbukan teaches Goju-Ryu karate-do, Kobudo and other related disciplines. For further information on seminars, visit www.bunbukan.com, or email bunbukan@hotmail.com.

GLOSSARY

Ashi Barai
foot sweep

Barate
back-of-the-fingers strike

Bu
martial, physical, body

Bu Do
martial way

Bun
mind, pen, literature, intellect, aesthetics

Bunbukan
place where the mental and the physical unite

Chudan
middle area

Chudan Uke
middle block

Dachi
stances

Do
way (path)

Dojo
training hall/place for seeking the way

Enso
circle/cyclic

Fudo Myoo
the immovable one

Gedan
lower area

Goju
hard/soft

Goju-Ryu
hard/soft school

Haito
ridge hand

Heiko Dachi
ready stance

Heishu
closed hand/fist

Hidari
left

Jo
place

Jodan
upper area

Ju
soft

Kake Uke
open hand hooking block

Kan
hall

GLOSSARY

Kaishu
open hand

Kaishu Chudan Hiki Uke
open hand pulling block to middle area

Kaishu Uke
open hand block

Karate
empty hand

Karate-Do
way of the empty hand

Kata
form

Ken To
two prominent knuckles of the fore fist

Kihon
basics

Kobudo
ancient martial way (weaponry)

Koken
back of the wrist/bent wrist

Koken Uke
wrist block

Maki Wara
striking post

Mawashi
circular

Mawashi Uke
circular block

Migi
right

Musabi Dachi
formal stance

Naote
closing/ending procedure

Nukite
finger strike

Otoshi
downward/descending

Rei
bow

Rei Shiki
etiquette

Renroku Waza
combination technique (drill)

Ryu
school (stream)

Sanchin
three battles

Sanchin Dachi
hour glass stance

Sanchin No Kamae
Sanchin opening stance

GLOSSARY

Seiken
fist

Seiza
sitting/kneeling in a meditative position

Shinto
way of the Kami (gods)

Shotei
palm heel

Shotei Oshi
palm heel push

Shotei Oshi Jodan
upper area palm heel push

Shotei Oshi Gedan
lower area palm heel push

Shotei Uke
palm heel block

Shuto Otoshi Uke
downward knife hand block

Shuto
knife hand

Tate
standing

Tensho
turning hands

Uchi
inner

Uchi Shotei
inner palm heel

Uchi Shotei Uke
inner palm heel block

Ushiro
back/rear

Ushiro Chudan Kake Uke
middle area inner hooking block

Ushiro Kake Uke
inner hooking block

Uke
blocks

Waza
technique

Yoi Dachi
ready stance

Yoko
side

Yoko Empi
side elbow strike

Yoko Koken
side/horizontal wrist block/strike

Yoko Koken Uke
outer wrist block

Also available from Summersdale

SHIHAN CHRIS ROWEN

THE SEMINARS

The first in the series of seminar DVD titles showcasing the Kata Tensho Karate of Shihan Chris Rowen.

VOLUME 1

DVD * REGION FREE * PAL

The Seminars Volume 1 (DVD)

Chris Rowen

£24.99

90 minutes

PAL all regions

This is the first in a series of DVDs recording the seminars of Shihan Chris Rowen, sixth dan – student of the legendary Hanshi Yamaguchi Gogen, tenth dan, and chief instructor of the Bunbukan Institute of Classical Japanese Budo Culture.

This DVD features Shihan Rowen's seminar at the first Ying and Yang of Karate conference in January 2005. The first of the seminars, it consists of a brief introduction to various martial arts subjects, which will be covered in more depth throughout the series. Includes principles of Ma-Maai (distance), Uke (blocks), Kaisitu Waza (open hand techniques) and covers circular moves/hooking, pulling and re-directing partner work and much more!

Goju-Ryu Karate-Do

KATA TENSHO

Ancient Form to Modern-Day Application

転掌

DVD * REGION FREE * PAL

Goju-Ryu Karate-Do Kata Tensho (DVD)

Ancient Form to Modern-Day Application

Chris Rowen

£24.99

PAL all regions

Tensho, which literally means 'turning hands', is one of the two main forms of the Goju school of karate-do. This DVD covers 500 years of the history of this form together with 160 step-by-step instructions for its use today.

BUNKAI-JUTSU

The Practical Application of Karate Kata

Iain Abernethy

Bunkai-Jutsu

The Practical Application of Karate Kata

Iain Abernethy

£17.99 Paperback

0 95389 321 9

Bunkai-jutsu is the analysis and application of the karate katas or 'forms' of karate in real combat. One of the most fascinating and misunderstood aspects of karate, this book explains the ethics of bunkai-jutsu and provides the reader with the information they need to unlock the 'secrets' of kata and to begin practising karate as the complete and realistic combat art that it was intended to be.

This groundbreaking book provides a detailed analysis of the combative concepts and principles upon which the katas are based.

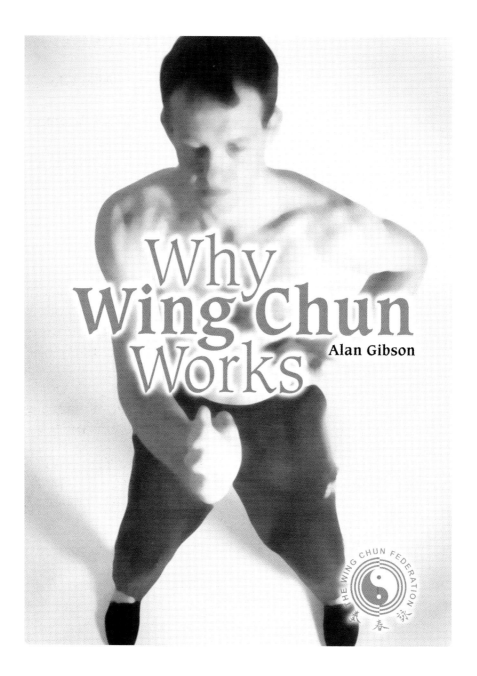

Why
Wing Chun
Works

Alan Gibson

THE WING CHUN FEDERATION

Why Wing Chun Works

Alan Gibson

£11.99 Paperback

1 84024 214 0

This highly popular and in depth study systematically explains all
the essential concepts, principles and basic training methods of the
Wing Chun system. Beautifully illustrated with easy to understand,
clear pictures and diagrams. Holistic health and philosophical
arguments are also fully covered.

Why Wing Chun Works is an essential training aid for anyone thinking
about or already studying Wing Chun. The Wing Chun system has
many logical and systematic learning methods; similarly this book is
divided into sections to facilitate the learning process. The book will
also prove invaluable for other experienced martial artists wishing
to broaden their horizons by studying different arts. This book
explains: how Wing Chun works; why it is so effective in practice;
and why its methods are so different to other arts.

Bushi-Jutsu

The Science of the Warrior

A Paskin & D Westwood

Bushi-Jutsu

The Science of the Warrior

Andy Paskin & Darren Westwood

£16.99 Paperback

0 95473 640 0

Bushi-Jutsu – The Science of the Warrior attempts to bridge the gap between the kata of old Okinawa, following the influence of the feudal Japanese militia, and that which is taught in today's dojo as 'effective' self-defence.

The distressing reality, for most kata bunkai students, is that there is very little 'real' application in the world today outside Japan. That which is taught as 'bunkai' tends to be *monkey-see-monkey-do* – very few really understand the highly technical and effective nature of this 'secret' part of karate.

This book by Andy Paskin and Darren Westwood doesn't just uncover the hidden nature of karate kata application – it literally rips the shroud of secrecy from around it and cleaves the mystery from it.

The book takes a pragmatic, sometimes controversial and always brutally honest look at modern karate as it is and as it was meant to be.

www.summersdale.com